How the World Celebrates

Celebrating Seasons

Around the World

Jennifer Kleiman

45TH PARALLEL PRESS

Published in the United States of America by Cherry Lake Publishing Group
Ann Arbor, Michigan
www.cherrylakepublishing.com

Reading Adviser: Beth Walker Gambro, MS, Ed., Reading Consultant, Yorkville, IL

Photo Credits: © Olga Strogonova/Dreamstime.com, cover, title page; © Evgeniy pavlovski/Dreamstime.com, 4; © Alexander Raths/Shutterstock, 6; © Raphael Comber Sales/Shutterstock, 7; © Chuta Kooanantkul/Shutterstock, 8; © Flower Studio/Shutterstock, 9; © Zhur_Sa/Shutterstock, 10; © romakoma/Shutterstock, 12; © DC Studio/Shutterstock, 13; © FG Trade/Shutterstock, 15; © Artistel/Shutterstock, 16; © Yulia Furman/Shutterstock, 19; © Piotr Wawrzyniuk/Shutterstock, 20; © JR P via Flickr CC BY-NC 2.0; © jiaming/Shutterstock, 24; © LilKar/Shutterstock, 26; © Tieu Tan Tan/Shutterstock, 27; © AstroStar/Shutterstock, 29

Copyright © 2025 by Cherry Lake Publishing Group
All rights reserved. No part of this book may be reproduced or utilized in any form or by any means without written permission from the publisher.

45th Parallel Press is an imprint of Cherry Lake Publishing Group.

Library of Congress Cataloging-in-Publication Data

Names: Kleiman, Jennifer, 1978- author.
Title: Celebrating seasons around the world / written by Jennifer Kleiman.
Description: Ann Arbor, MI : 45th Parallel Press, 2025. | Series: How the world celebrates | Audience: Grades 4-6 | Summary: "From festivals of light in the dark days of winter to harvest celebrations, cultures around the world celebrate the joys each season brings in different ways. Readers will explore the customs and traditions that define those celebrations. This hi-lo narrative nonfiction series celebrates diverse cultures while highlighting how expressions of joy and connection are all part of the human experience"-- Provided by publisher.
Identifiers: LCCN 2024036515 | ISBN 9781668956595 (hardcover) | ISBN 9781668957448 (paperback) | ISBN 9781668958315 (ebook) | ISBN 9781668959183 (pdf)
Subjects: LCSH: Festivals--Juvenile literature. | Seasons--Juvenile literature.
Classification: LCC GT3933 .K57 2025 | DDC 394.26--dc23/eng/20240918
LC record available at https://lccn.loc.gov/2024036515

Cherry Lake Publishing would like to acknowledge the work of the Partnership for 21st Century Learning, a network of Battelle for Kids. Please visit Battelle for Kids online for more information.

Printed in the United States of America

NOTE FROM PUBLISHER: Websites change regularly, and their future contents are outside of our control. Supervise children when conducting any recommended online searches for extended learning opportunities.

Table of Contents

INTRODUCTION **5**

CHAPTER 1:
HOLIDAY SEASON IN THE UNITED STATES **11**

CHAPTER 2:
A HINDU FESTIVAL OF COLORS **17**

CHAPTER 3:
A SCANDINAVIAN MIDSUMMER **21**

CHAPTER 4:
A CHINESE MID-AUTUMN FESTIVAL **25**

ACTIVITY:
MAKING COLOR POWDER FOR HOLI **30**

LEARN MORE **31**
GLOSSARY **32**
INDEX **32**
ABOUT THE AUTHOR **32**

DID YOU KNOW? The summer **solstice** is the longest day of the year. It happens around June 21. The winter solstice marks the shortest day. It happens around December 21.

Introduction

Winter. Spring. Summer. Fall. These are the seasons that make up a year. Each season lasts about 3 months. This is due to Earth's tilted **axis**. An axis is an imaginary line. Earth rotates around it. Picture a pole going through the center of Earth. Now imagine the pole is tilted a bit. As the Earth spins, it tilts too. This causes parts of Earth to get more sun. These are the long, hot days of summer. When it's titled away, we get winter. The days are shorter and colder.

The seasons are closely linked to life on Earth. They reflect the cycle of life. Spring is a time for birth. Animals are born. Plants spring back to life. In fact, "springtime" comes from this idea. It is the time when plants spring from the soil. It is time to celebrate new life.

Summer is a time for growth. The long, hot days of summer are perfect for this. Animals grow and leave the nest. Fruits and vegetables grow and ripen. There is plenty of food to eat. We celebrate the warm weather. We spend time outdoors.

Fall is a time to prepare for winter. The days get shorter. The air is cooler. We **harvest**, or gather, crops. Animals gather food too. We celebrate what nature has given us. Fall is also called autumn.

Winter is a time to rest. Even nature rests. Plants become **dormant**. They stop growing. Animals **hibernate**, or sleep. People rest too. We take breaks from school and work. We spend time indoors with loved ones. It is a time to celebrate togetherness.

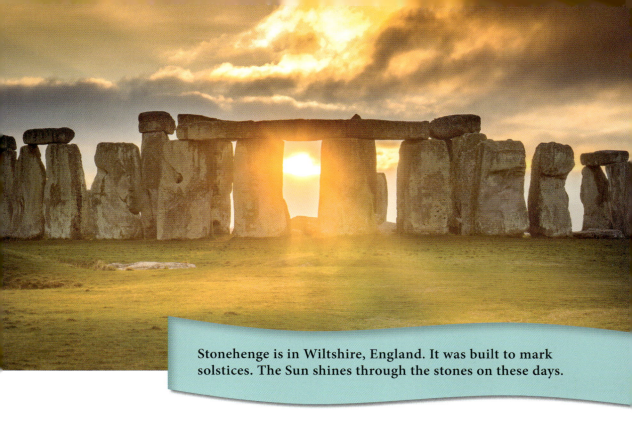

Stonehenge is in Wiltshire, England. It was built to mark solstices. The Sun shines through the stones on these days.

THE HISTORY OF CELEBRATING SEASONS

Human life is closely connected to the seasons. So is human culture. Nearly every religion has seasonal celebrations. They are also the basis for our earliest religions.

Before farming, people hunted and gathered. Changing seasons meant changing food sources. People celebrated with **ritual** feasts. A ritual is a religious ceremony. They gave thanks to the gods. These were gods who controlled nature.

Akitu was an important spring festival in ancient Mesopotamia. It marked the new year. It celebrated rebirth. Ruins like this one of the Mesopotamian city of Dara help us learn about the past.

Seasonal **traditions** evolved as societies grew. A tradition is a behavior passed down over time. People began farming. Seasons became even more important. A poor harvest could mean starvation. A good harvest was a reason to give thanks. Special days were set aside for feasting and **fasting**. Fasting means not eating. Seasonal festivals became a tradition. They included singing, dancing, rituals, and prayer. They honored nature. They celebrated the seasons.

Today, some of these seasonal celebrations remain. New ones have emerged. Celebrating the seasons is part of human culture. These celebrations remind us to be thankful. They are an opportunity to celebrate life.

The **HOLIDAY SEASON** takes place in North America. It falls between the U.S. Thanksgiving and New Year. The season includes festivals from different cultures and religions. Christmas, Hanukkah, and Kwanzaa are included. This reflects the rich diversity of American culture.

Chapter 1
Holiday Season in the United States

Everyone is in a festive mood. It is the last day of school. Tomorrow, winter break begins. Joy's class is doing a white elephant gift exchange. Everyone brings a small wrapped gift. They place them in a pile. Each student draws a number. They pick a gift in order of their numbers. They can choose to keep the gift or swap it. Joy unwraps a paint set. Dimitri's turn is next. He chooses to swap with Joy. He is an artist. He trades her his book. Each student also brings a gift for the holiday toy drive. The drive collects toys for kids in need.

A wonderful surprise awaits Joy after school. "Kwame!"

Joy's brother has come to pick her up. He is home from college.

"How long are you home?"

"Until Christmas," he replies. "Then I am going to Hadah's for Kwanzaa." Hadah is Kwame's girlfriend.

"I made Hadah a card," Joy says. "I made you one too." Kwame's card wishes him a Merry Christmas. Hadah's wishes her a Happy Kwanzaa.

Kwame hugs his sister. "Thank you, Joy."

Kwame plays holiday music on the drive home. Joy admires the decorations. Many homes are covered in twinkling lights. Joy hums along to the music. She is getting into the holiday spirit.

Mama and Joy are doing their holiday shopping. The holiday spirit is everywhere. Strangers wish one another "Happy Holidays." Shoppers hold the doors for each other. A man dressed as Santa Claus rings a bell. He is collecting money for charity. Joy gives him a dollar.

"That was kind of you," says Mama.

Joy smiles. "I'm in the giving spirit."

THE HOLIDAYS

Christmas is a Christian holiday. It is traditionally celebrated for 12 days. It lasts from Christmas Day to the Epiphany, or 3 Kings' Day. It celebrates the birth of Jesus of Nazareth. He is called Jesus Christ. Christmas is celebrated with giving and generosity. Families gather.

Hanukkah is the Jewish Festival of Light. It lasts 8 days. A candle is lit each day. It is lit on a Hanukkah. That is a type of menorah. It holds 9 candles. This holiday celebrates a miracle from long ago. Jewish fighters risked their lives. They defeated a Greek army. They only had enough sacred oil for 1 night. But that oil lasted 8 nights! It lasted until more arrived. The holy lamp did not go out.

Kwanzaa is a special African American holiday. It is **secular**. Secular means not religious. It celebrates Black culture and values. Kwanzaa lasts for 7 days. Each day honors a principle of Kwanzaa. A candle is lit each day.

The 7 principles are:
1. *Umoja* (unity)
2. *Kujichagulia* (**self-determination**, or deciding for oneself)
3. *Ujima* (**collective**, or whole group, work and responsibility)
4. *Ujamaa* (cooperative economics)
5. *Nia* (purpose)
6. *Kuumba* (creativity)
7. *Imani* (faith)

On Christmas Day, the streets are quiet. Most businesses are closed. Everyone is home. Outside, it is snowing. The world is still.

Joy's family exchanges gifts. They watch holiday movies. They sip hot cocoa. Family members come over for dinner. Joy's father has baked a ham. Her mother has made fruitcake.

After dinner, everyone lingers. There is nowhere to go. People talk and laugh. They play games. This is the part that Joy enjoys most. Everyone is together. Everyone is happy. Everyone is thankful. It is the best part of the holiday season.

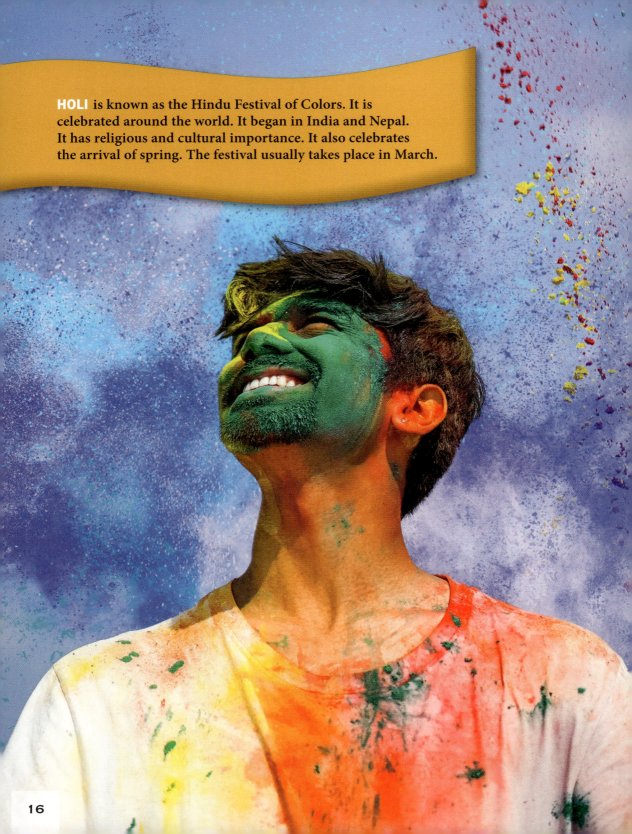

HOLI is known as the Hindu Festival of Colors. It is celebrated around the world. It began in India and Nepal. It has religious and cultural importance. It also celebrates the arrival of spring. The festival usually takes place in March.

Chapter 2
A Hindu Festival of Colors

"*Holi hai!*" cries Tamil. "It's Holi!"

Tamil throws fistfuls of colored powder into the air. Others do the same. The air is a dusty rainbow of colors. Only moments before, people's clothes were white. Now, they wear the colors of spring.

Balloons filled with colored water soar over balconies. "Holi hai!" cries Tamil's brother. A balloon breaks over Tamil's head.

"I will get you, Rohan!" Tamil grabs a water gun. It is filled with colored water. The water symbolizes the arrival of spring.

Tamil chases his brother through the streets. Everywhere, there is music and color. Everywhere, there is joy. It is Holi! It is spring!

Tamil and Rohan wash themselves. Guests will soon arrive. The boys are eager to greet them. Uncle is first. Tamil smears a dab of yellow on Uncle's cheeks.

"For good health, Uncle."

Tamil and Rohan take turns. The boys pick out colors for each guest.

Tamil's cousin Munira arrives. They've been fighting recently. Tamil rubs an orange streak across Munira's cheek. Orange symbolizes forgiveness. It means new beginnings. It is tradition to forgive past wrongs on Holi.

DID YOU KNOW?

Spring is harvest time in India. Many farmers harvest grains, such as wheat, and lentils. These are winter crops. People light bonfires on the eve of Holi. They roast a blend of these grains. The blend is called *holaka*. It's where Holi comes from.

The colors seen during Holi symbolize different things. Green symbolizes spring and rebirth. Yellow symbolizes joy and health. Red symbolizes **fertility**. Fertility means the ability to produce plants or offspring. Fertile soil produces many crops.

    A table is set with traditional Holi snacks. The *pakoras* are Tamil's favorite. They are a type of fritter. They are crispy and delicious. Rohan sips *thandai*. It is a sweet milk drink.

    Outside, music fills the air. Guests dance to traditional Holi songs. Tamil's cousin plays the *dohl*. It is a type of drum. People laugh and rejoice. They welcome the season of hope and new beginnings!

MIDSUMMER is a national holiday in Sweden and Finland. It takes place in June on or near the summer solstice. This began as a **pagan** celebration. A pagan religion worships many gods.

Chapter 3
A Scandinavian Midsummer

Elsa wakes up early to pick wildflowers. Her bare feet are wet with morning dew. Midsummer dew is said to have healing powers. Elsa will weave the flowers into crowns for guests. Wearing them is a Midsummer tradition. She will also make a wreath for the maypole.

Pappa and Bjorn are raising the maypole. It is 20 feet (6 meters) tall. It is decorated in flowers and greenery. They use ropes and pulleys to help raise it.

Mamma and Annika, Bjorn's wife, make food. They are preparing the **smorgasbord**. This is like a buffet. It is filled with traditional Swedish foods. Mamma lays out an assortment of bread and cheese. There is pickled herring and cured salmon.

There are potatoes with dill and sour cream. Annika has made meatballs. There are also lots of fresh strawberries. No Midsummer would be complete without strawberries and cream.

After lunch, it is time for the Maypole Dance. All the guests gather around the pole. They start with the "Little Frogs" dance. It is one of the most popular songs during Midsummer. Everyone dances in circles, pretending to be frogs. They sing while they dance. It is fun and silly. People of all ages take part. It's what Midsummer is all about.

DID YOU KNOW?

Midsummer is usually celebrated in the countryside. Towns and cities are deserted. Businesses are closed. Noisy cities become quiet.

This painting was made in 1915 by artist Nikolai Astrup. The Midsummer festival has a long tradition of joy and community togetherness.

It is a beautiful Midsummer evening. The guests gather for a bonfire by the sea. Elsa has collected firewood for days. The fires were once said to ward off evil spirits. Elsa thinks it must be working. She sees only joy and togetherness. Some people are playing music and singing. Others are talking. The children are playing games. It is loud and cheerful. Making noise is part of the Midsummer tradition. It brings luck for the year.

The **MID-AUTUMN FESTIVAL** is an ancient harvest festival. It honors the Moon. It is also called the Moon Festival or Mooncake Festival. It is celebrated based on the traditional Chinese calendar. It takes place on a full Moon. It usually falls in September or October. It is one of the most important Chinese holidays.

Chapter 4
A Chinese Mid-Autumn Festival

Chen and Ma rise early to make mooncakes. They will give boxes of them as gifts. Giving gifts of mooncakes is a Mid-Autumn Festival tradition. They symbolize family reunion. Family reunion is the most important part of the day. Soon, their home will be filled with family. Some are traveling from very far. Chen's aunt is flying all the way from London, England.

Ma wraps the dough around a ball of lotus paste. She rolls it in her palms. Chen presses the ball into the mooncake mold. This molds the dough into shape. The result is beautiful. The ball turns into a small round cake. It reminds Chen of a full Moon. An image of the Moon Rabbit is pressed into the top.

RABBIT ON THE MOON

The Moon Rabbit is based on a Chinese legend. It comes from markings on the Moon. The markings are shaped like a rabbit. Moon legends are associated with the Mid-Autumn Festival. Some legends are about Buddha. Buddha is a Chinese religious leader.

In this legend, Buddha disguised himself as a hungry old man. He approached a fox, a monkey, and a rabbit. He asked for food. The fox caught a fish. The monkey brought some fruit. The rabbit had nothing to offer. So he threw himself into the fire. He offered himself as meat. In gratitude, Buddha brought the rabbit back to life. He sent him to the Moon to be worshiped.

In the afternoon, the house is filled with people. Chen and her cousins make paper lanterns. Lanterns are an important part of the Mid-Autumn Festival. They light people's way to good fortune. Chen and her cousins will hang them outside. They will light them when it's dark.

Laughter drifts from the kitchen. Ma and Chen's aunts are preparing dinner. They are making roast duck and sticky rice dumplings. They roast pumpkins. Everyone has brought mooncakes to share.

After dinner, it is time for Moon-gazing. It is a Mid-Autumn Festival tradition. It is when the Moon is the brightest and roundest.

Everyone is outside. Blankets are spread on the ground. Strings of paper lanterns sway gently in the breeze. Chen's aunts pass around boxes of mooncakes. Chen and her cousin Mei lie on their backs. The girls laugh and tell secrets. They take small bites of the sweet cakes. They stare at the Moon. The Moon gazes back, full and bright.

DID YOU KNOW?

Mooncakes may have helped free China from the Mongols. Stories say that plans for **revolts** were hidden in mooncakes. A revolt is when people rebel. They rebel against people in power. Mooncakes were given as gifts to supporters.

ACTIVITY: MAKING COLOR POWDER FOR HOLI

Want to make your own Holi color powder? All you need are some basic ingredients.

MATERIALS:

- 1 cup (20 mL) cornstarch
- 1/3 cup (80 mL) room-temperature water
- Mixing bowl
- Mixing spoon
- Liquid food color
- Baking sheet

INSTRUCTIONS:

1. In the bowl, use the spoon to mix the cornstarch and the water.
2. Add your favorite liquid food color. Get creative. Try mixing different colors.
3. Transfer the mixture to a baking sheet. Let it dry for 2 days. It should turn into a brick.
4. Break it up. You are now ready to throw a Holi party!

LEARN MORE

BOOKS:
Bentley, Joyce. *Happy Holi: The Festival of Colour.* London, England: Wayland, 2018.

Kaminski, Leah. *Nǐ Hǎo,* China. Ann Arbor, MI: Cherry Lake Publishing, 2020.

Orr, Tamra B. *Indian Heritage.* Ann Arbor, MI: Cherry Lake Publishing, 2018.

ONLINE:
With an adult, explore more online with these suggested searches.

- "Holi Hai!" The Hindu American Foundation
- "Mid-Autumn Festival story and how Chinese celebrate it," China Highlights via YouTube
- "Små Grodorna: Swedish Midsummer Song – Lyrics & English Translation," Hej Sweden

GLOSSARY

axis (AK-suhs) an imaginary line around which a shape rotates

collective (kuh-LEK-tiv) relating to a group as a whole, marked by cooperation and sharing

dormant (DOR-muhnt) asleep or inactive

fasting (FAA-sting) to purposely not eat for a period of time

fertility (fuhr-TIH-luh-tee) ability to produce, as in crops or offspring

harvest (HAR-vuhst) the process of gathering crops

hibernate (HIE-buhr-nayt) to pass the winter in a resting state

pagan (PAY-guhn) having to do with a religion that worships many gods

revolts (rih-VOLTS) uprisings against someone or something, usually armed

ritual (RIH-chuh-wuhl) a ceremonial act

secular (SHE-kyoo-ler) not religious

self-determination (SELF dih-ter-muh-NAY-shuhn) the ability to choose freely

smorgasbord (SMOR-guhs-bord) a buffet with a variety of foods and dishes

solstice (SOHL-stus) the shortest and longest days of the year

traditions (truh-DIH-shuhnz) practices passed down over time

INDEX

Akitu, 8
autumn, 6, 24–29

Buddha, 26

celebrations, 7, 8, 9, 10–15, 16–19, 20–23, 24–28, 30
China, 24–28
Christmas, 10, 11–13, 14, 15

Earth's rotation, 5

fall, 6, 24–29
family, 15, 18, 25, 27
Finland, 20–23

food, 6, 7, 9, 15, 18, 19, 21–22, 24, 25, 27, 28

gifts, 11, 13, 14, 15, 25, 28

Hanukkah, 10, 14
harvests and farming, 6, 7, 9, 18, 24
Hindu festivals, 16–19
Holi, 16–19, 30

India, 16–19, 30

Jewish holidays, 10, 14

Kwanzaa, 10, 11–12, 14

Mid-Autumn Festival, 24–29
Midsummer, 20–23
Moon Festival, 24–29

Nepal, 16–19
North America, 10–15

rituals and festivals, 7, 8, 9, 10–15, 16–19, 20–23, 24–28, 30

Scandinavian holidays, 20–23
solstices, 4, 7, 20
spring, 5, 16–19
summer, 4, 6, 20–23
summer solstice, 4, 20
Sweden, 20–23

traditions, 9, 14, 18, 21–23, 28

United States, 10–15

winter, 6, 10–15
winter solstice, 4

ABOUT THE AUTHOR

Jennifer Kleiman has worked in educational publishing for more than 20 years. Today, she is a busy writer and editor, working on her second novel. She lives in Chicago, in a rickety old house, with her wife, 2 cats, a dog named Helen, and a yard full of chickens.